Welcome to Our World

SECOND EDITION

Series Editors
Joan Kang Shin & JoAnn (Jodi) Crandall

Authors
Jill Korey O'Sullivan & Joan Kang Shin

NATIONAL GEOGRAPHIC
LEARNING

Australia • Brazil • Canada • Mexico • Singapore • United Kingdom • United States

Scope and Sequence

Can You Help Me? p. 4

Requests, Polite language
Song: Can You Help Me?

Language in Use: Can you help me, please? Yes, I can.   Thank you. You're welcome.
Can I have the [book], please? Yes.   Thanks. You're welcome.

	1 Table, Scissors, Crayons p. 8	**2** Let's Play p. 16	**3** I Like Rice p. 24	**4** Animals on the Farm p. 32
Theme	Classroom Objects	Play Time	Food / Snacks	Farm Animals
Vocabulary	a chair a box a computer scissors a crayon a table a pencil	a seesaw climb a slide jump a swing play run	beans milk cheese rice chocolate yoghurt eggs	a chicken a duck a cow a goat a donkey a horse
Song	Where's the Crayon?	What Can You Do?	The Rice Pudding Song	Ali Baba's Got a Big Farm
The Sounds of English	/t/ table /t/ tall /t/ tortoise /t/ two	/ʌ/ run /ʌ/ sun /ʌ/ up /ʌ/ mummy	/tʃ/ cheese /tʃ/ chair /tʃ/ chocolate	/k/ cow /k/ duck /k/ computer /k/ chicken /k/ cat
Concepts	in, on, under	up / down	black, brown, white	6, 7
Language in Use	(Receptive: Where's the [book]?) It's on the [table].	(Receptive: What can you do?) I can [jump].	(Receptive: Do you like [yoghurt]?) Yes, I do. / No, I don't.	(Receptive: How many [horses] are there?) There are [3 horses].
Project	Make a pencil holder.	Make a seesaw.	Make a bean shaker.	Make a duck mask.

Units 1–4 Review / Game   pp. 40–41

Welcome to Our WORLD 2

SECOND EDITION

	5 **Shorts and Jumpers** p. 42	**6** **I Can See a Bee** p. 50	**7** **I'm Happy** p. 58	**8** **Boats, Cars, Bikes** p. 66

Theme	Clothes	Nature	Feelings	Transport
Vocabulary	boots sandals a coat shorts a hat a T-shirt a jumper	an ant a ladybird a bee a leaf a butterfly a rock a caterpillar	angry crying happy laughing sad smiling tired	an aeroplane a car a bike a fire engine a boat a motorbike a bus
Song	I've Got a Little Doll	Oh, Butterfly!	If You're Happy and You Know It	Tiny Little Boat
The Sounds of English	/h/ hat /h/ horse /h/ hand /h/ hair	/ɒ/ rock /ɒ/ doll /ɒ/ box /ɒ/ socks	/l/ laughing /l/ leaf /l/ ladybird	/aɪ/ fire engine /aɪ/ slide /aɪ/ smiling /aɪ/ rice
Concepts	hot / cold	8, 9, 10	same / different	fast / slow
Language in Use	(Receptive: Are you wearing [boots]?) Yes, I am. / No, I'm not.	I can see [a butterfly].	(Receptive: How do you feel?) I'm [angry]!	(Receptive: Are [bikes] fast?) Yes, they are. / No, they aren't.
Project	Make a winter hat.	Make a butterfly.	Make a happy / sad puppet.	Make an aeroplane.

Units 5–8 Review / Game   pp. 74–75

Can You Help Me?

BIG Frog

Can you help me, please?

Yes, I can.

Look and listen. Say. **TR: 0.2**

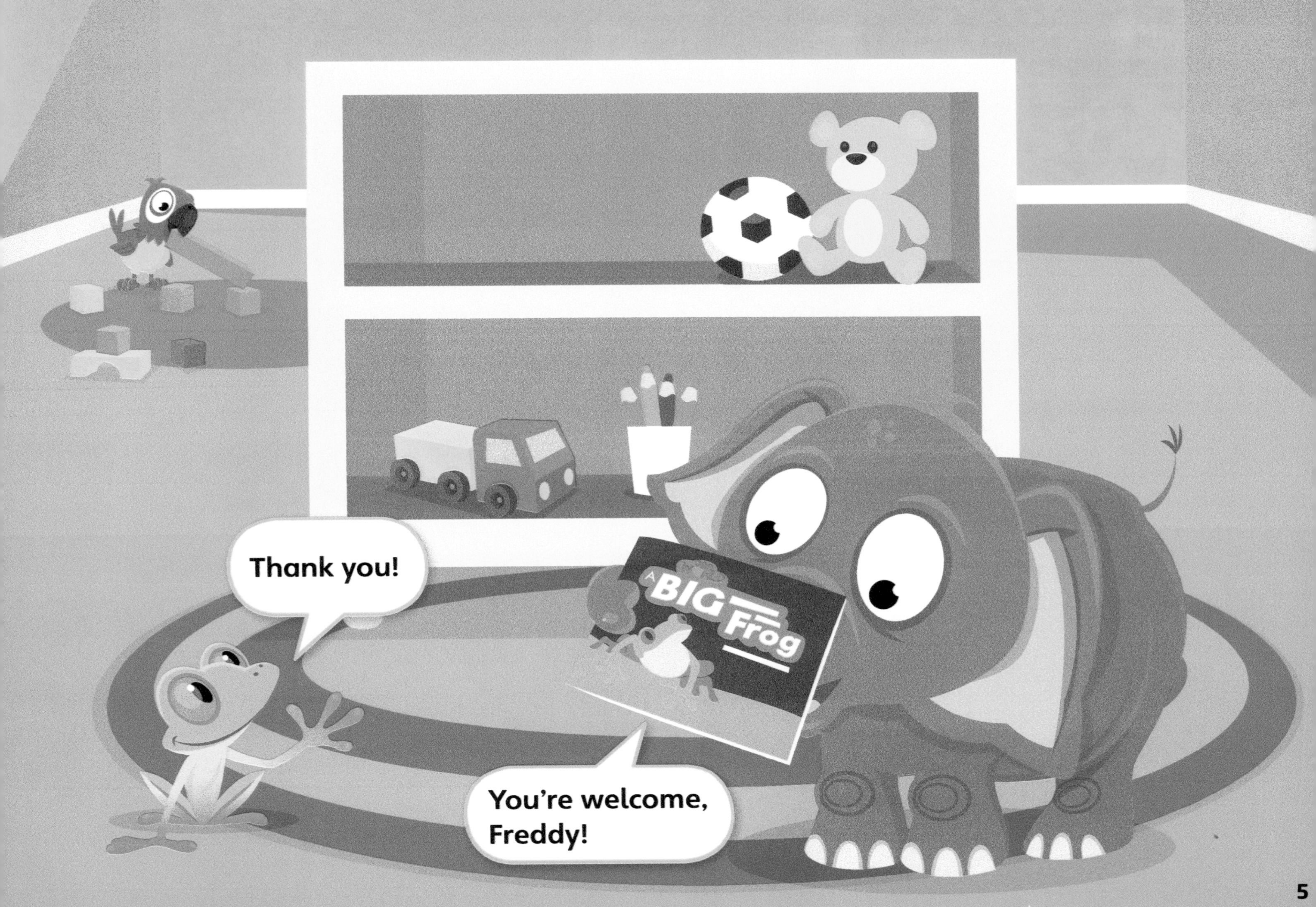

Can I have the book, please?

Yes.

Thanks, Freddy!

You're welcome, Mia.

1 Table, Scissors, Crayons

Listen, point and say. TR: 1.1
Listen and say. TR: 1.2

A girl drawing in India

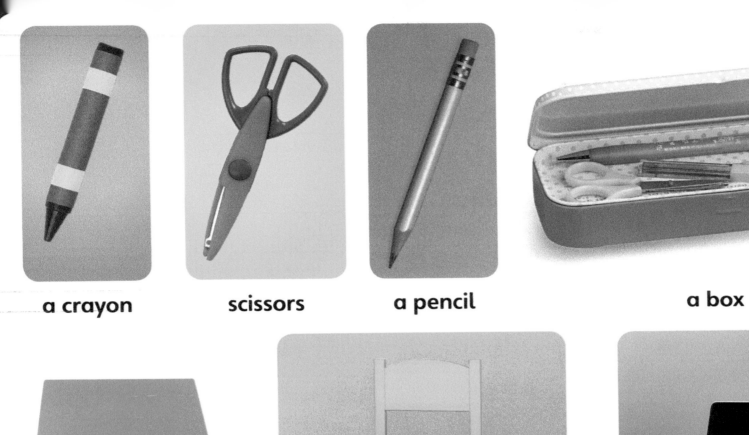

a crayon   **scissors**   **a pencil**   **a box**

a table   **a chair**   **a computer**

on

in

under

PRACTICE Say and colour.

PROJECT Make a pencil holder.

2 Let's Play

Listen, point and say. TR: 2.1

Listen and say. TR: 2.2

A boy on a tyre swing in the USA

a swing

a slide

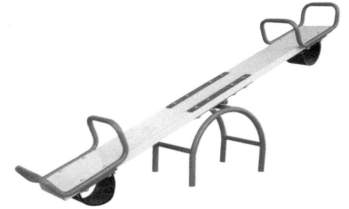

a seesaw

jump

play

run

climb

up

down

Squirrels on a tree

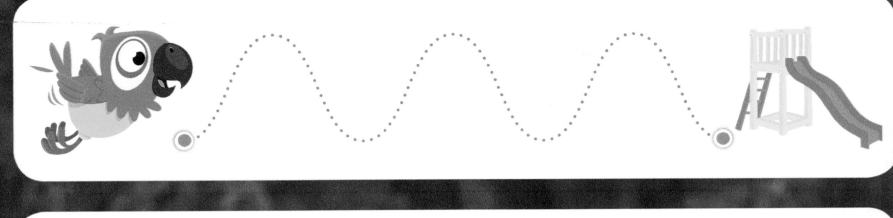

PROJECT Make a seesaw.

3 I Like Rice

Listen, point and say. TR: 3.1

Listen and say. TR: 3.2

Bears made from rice in Japan

rice

cheese

beans

chocolate

yoghurt

milk

eggs

black

white

brown

Three chickens

PROJECT Make a bean shaker.

4 Animals on the Farm

Listen, point and say. TR: 4.1

Listen and say. TR: 4.2a

Young goats on a
horse in Germany

a chicken

a cow

a horse

a donkey

a duck

a goat

6

Six ducklings

7

Seven ducklings

PROJECT Make a duck mask.

REVIEW Listen and draw lines. TR: 4.7

5 Shorts and Jumpers

Listen, point and say. TR: 5.1

Listen and say. TR: 5.2a

A girl on an ice
slide in China

a hat

a coat

boots

a jumper

sandals

a T-shirt

shorts

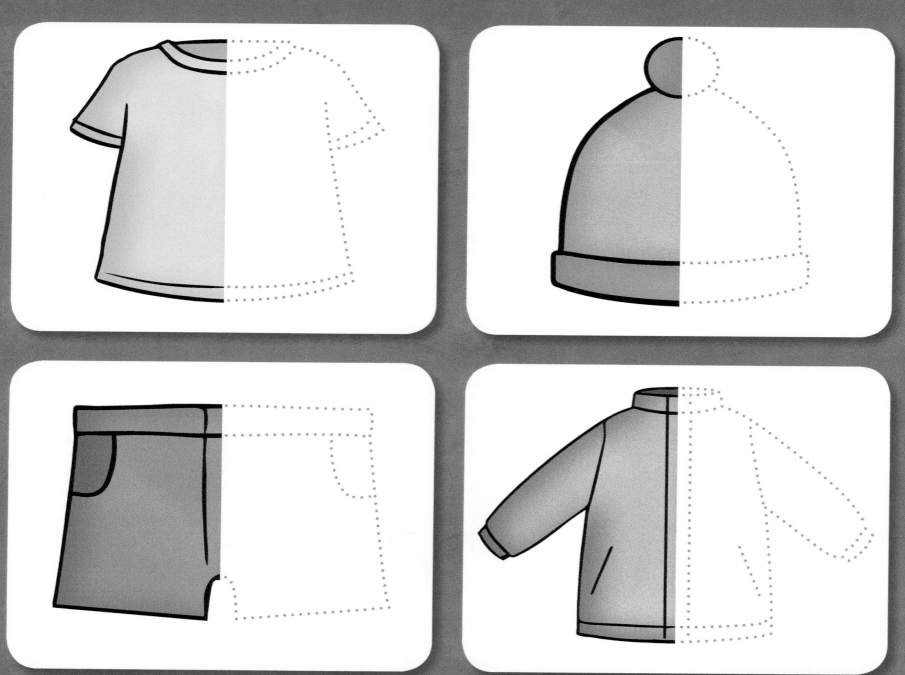

hot

cold

Fuego volcano in Guatemala

K2 (Chogori),
Karakoram mountain range

PROJECT Make a winter hat.

I Can See a Bee

Listen, point and say. TR: 6.1

Listen and say. TR: 6.2

A bee near purple flowers in the USA

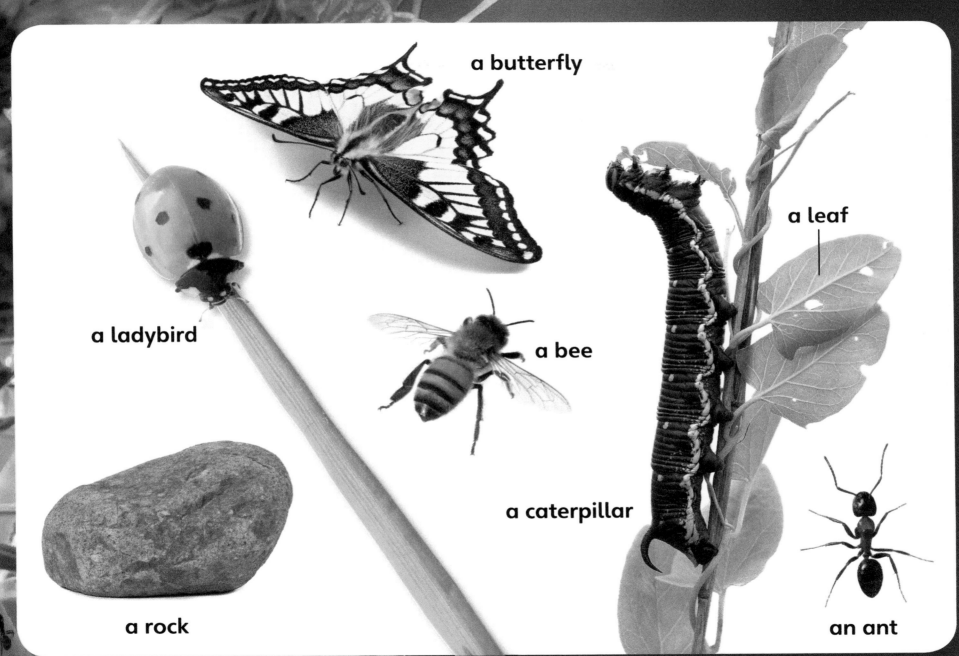

a butterfly

a leaf

a ladybird

a bee

a caterpillar

a rock

an ant

51

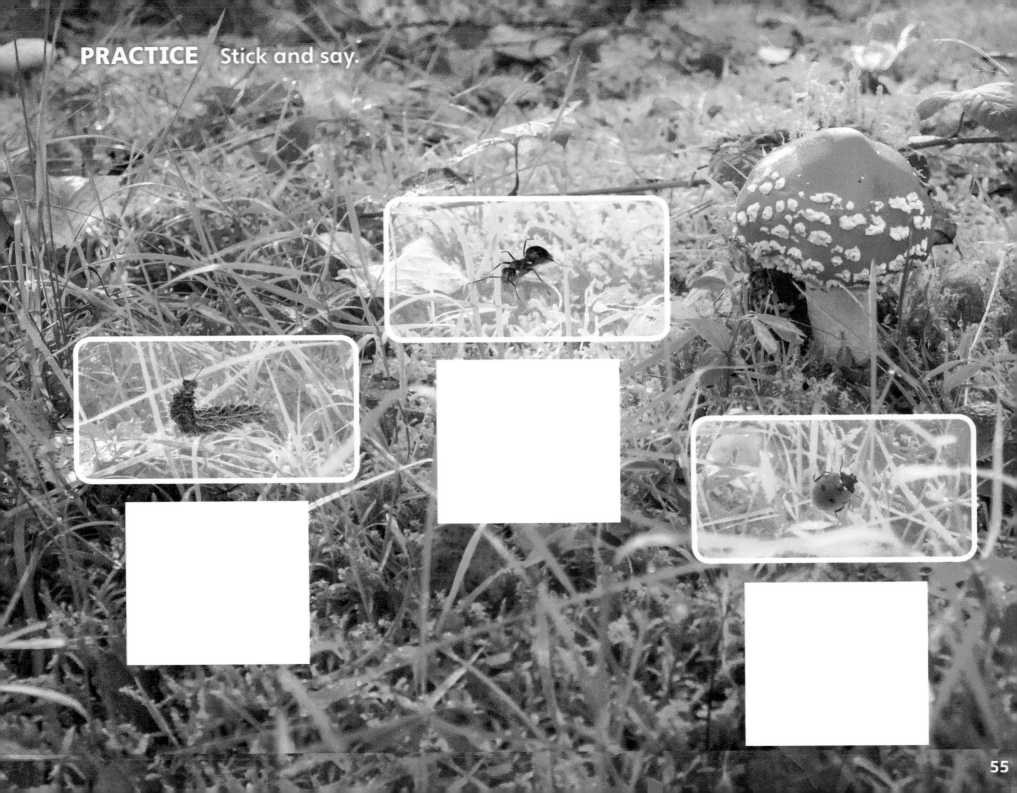

PROJECT   Make a butterfly.

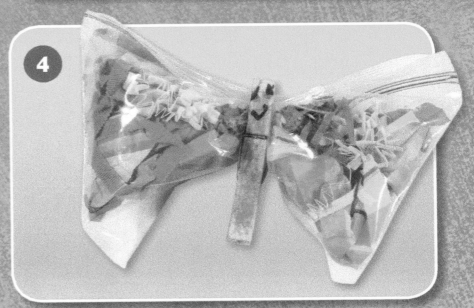

Listen, point and say. TR: 7.1

Listen and say. TR: 7.2a

Happy children, Taz Peninsula in Russia

VOCABULARY Listen, point and say. TR: 7.3

happy

laughing

smiling

tired

sad

crying

angry

same

Two frogs

A frog and a snail

different

PROJECT   Make a happy / sad puppet.

Boats, Cars, Bikes

Listen, point and say. TR: 8.1

Listen and say. TR: 8.2

A boy riding in his toy car in Kosovo

an aeroplane

a bike

a boat

a bus

a car

a motorbike

a fire engine

PRACTICE Circle. Say the words.

fast

A cheetah in Kenya

A leopard tortoise in South Africa

slow

PROJECT   Make an aeroplane.

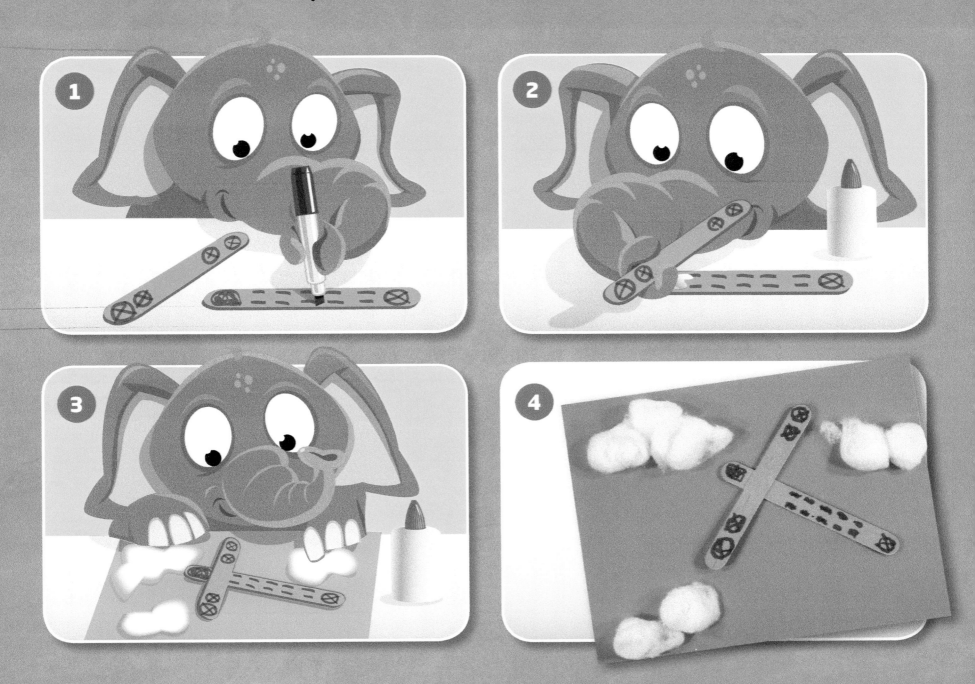

GAME   Play and say.

The Alphabet TR: A–Z

A apple

B bird

C cat

D dog

I insect

J juice

K king

L lion

Q queen

R rabbit

S socks

T train

U umbrella

E egg

F fire engine

G goat

H hand

M milk

N nose

O orange

P puzzle

V violin

W window

X box

Y yoghurt

Z zebra

I Can ...

1 I can talk about my classroom.

2 I can talk about playing.

3 I can talk about food.

4 I can talk about farm animals.

5 I can talk about clothes.

6 I can talk about nature.

7 I can talk about my feelings.

8 I can talk about transport.

Chant and Song Lyrics

SONG TR: 0.5 p.7
Can You Help Me?

Can you help me?
Can you help me?
Yes, I can.
Yes, I can.
Can I have the book, please?
Can I have the book, please?
Here it is.
Here it is.

Thank you!
You're welcome!

1

CHANT TR: 1.2 p.8

Crayon. Crayon.
Can I have the crayon?
Crayon. Crayon.
Look, it's in the box.
Pencil. Pencil.
Can I have the pencil?
Pencil. Pencil.
Look, it's in the box.

1

SONG TR: 1.4 p.11
Where's the Crayon?

Where's the crayon?
La di da di da di da di!
Where's the crayon?
La di da di da di dum – dim dum!

It's on the chair.
La di da di da di da di!
It's on the chair.
La di da di da di dum – dim dum!

Where's the chair?
La di da di da di da di!
Where's the chair?
La di da di da di dum – dim dum!

It's under the table.
La di da di da di da di!
It's under the table.
La di da di da di dum – dim dum!

Where's the table?
La di da di da di da di!
Where's the table?
La di da di da di dum – dim dum!

It's right here!
La di da di da di da di!
It's right here!
La di da di da di dum – dim dum!

Chant and Song Lyrics

2 **CHANT** TR: 2.2 p.16

Swing, swing, I'm on the swing.
Swing, swing, I'm on the swing.
Wheeeeeeee!

Slide, slide. I'm on the slide.
Slide, slide, I'm on the slide.
Wheeeeeeeee!

Seesaw, seesaw, I'm on the seesaw.
Seesaw, seesaw, I'm on the seesaw.
Wheeeeeee!

2 **SONG** TR: 2.4 p.19
What Can You Do?

What can you do? What can you do?
What can you do? What can you do?

I can run around the playground with you.
I can run around the playground with you.
What can you do? What can you do?
What can you do? What can you do?

I can jump around the playground with you.
I can jump around the playground with you.
What can you do? What can you do?
What can you do? What can you do?

I can climb around the playground with you.
I can climb around the playground with you.
What can you do? What can you do?
What can you do? What can you do?

I can dance around the playground with you.
I can dance around the playground with you.
What can you do? What can you do?
What can you do? What can you do?

Chant and Song Lyrics

3

CHANT TR: 3.2 p.24

Rice, please. Rice, please.
Rice, rice, rice, please.
Beans, please. Beans, please.
Bean, beans, beans, please.
Cheese, please. Cheese, please.
Cheese, cheese, cheese, please.

Rice, beans, cheese.
Rice, beans, cheese.
Rice, beans, cheese.
Please, please, please.

3

SONG TR: 3.4 p.27
The Rice Pudding Song

[Repeat each line two times.]

Rice, rice pudding! I like it!
First you get the milk, and you pour it, you pour it.

Rice, rice pudding! I like it!
Then you get the sugar, and you mix it, you mix it.

Rice, rice pudding! I like it!
Then you get the rice, and you cook it, you cook it.

Rice, rice pudding! I like it!
Then you get the egg, and you beat it, you beat it.

Rice, rice pudding! I like it!
Then you get it all, and you mix it, you mix it.

Rice, rice pudding! I like it!
Then you get the pudding, and you eat it, you eat it!

Mm mm mm mm mm mm!
Mm mm mm!

Chant and Song Lyrics

4 CHANT TR: 4.2a p.32

On the farm, farm, farm, farm.
There's a horse, horse, horse, horse.
Neigh, neigh, neigh, neigh, neigh, neigh.
Neigh, neigh, neigh, neigh, neigh, neigh.

On the farm, farm, farm, farm.
There's a goat, goat, goat, goat.
Baa, baa, baa, baa, baa, baa.
Baa, baa, baa, baa, baa, baa.

4 SONG TR: 4.4 p.35

Ali Baba's Got a Big Farm

Ali Baba, he's got a big farm.
On his farm there are seven cows. 1-2-3-4-5-6-7 cows. Moo!
All on Ali Baba's big farm.

Ali Baba, he's got a big farm.
On his farm there are seven goats. 1-2-3-4-5-6-7 goats. Baa!
All on Ali Baba's big farm.

Ali Baba, he's got a big farm.
On his farm there are seven ducks. 1-2-3-4-5-6-7 ducks. Quack!
All on Ali Baba's big farm.

Chant and Song Lyrics

5

CHANT TR: 5.2a p. 42

Hat, hat. Where is the hat?
Hat, hat. It's on my head!

Coat, coat. Where is the coat?
Coat, coat. It's on my body!

Boots, boots. Where are the boots?
Boots, boots. They're on my feet!

5

SONG TR: 5.4 p. 45
I've Got a Little Doll

I've got a little doll.
She is wearing blue,
Little blue trousers and a T-shirt, too.
Little doll, it is very cold for you.
Wear your blue boots and your jumper, too.

I've got a little doll.
She is wearing blue,
Little blue boots and a jumper, too.
Little doll, it is very cold for you.
Wear your blue coat and your blue hat, too.

I've got a little doll.
She is wearing blue.
Little blue coat and a blue hat, too.
Little doll, it is not cold for you.
With blue boots, jumper, coat and a blue hat, too!

Chant and Song Lyrics

6 **CHANT** TR: 6.2 p.50

Bee, bee, bee
Where's the bee?
Bee, bee, bee
Where's the bee?
Look on the rock.
It isn't there.
Look on the leaf.
It isn't there.
Look on the flower.
There's the bee!

6 **SONG** TR: 6.4 p.53
Oh, Butterfly!

Oh, butterfly, you are so beautiful.
Orange and black, you are so beautiful.
You love the flower.
The flower loves you.
Flying around.
We all love you, too.

Oh, ladybird, you are so beautiful.
Red and black, you are so beautiful.
You love the flower.
The flower loves you.
Flying around.
We all love you, too.

Oh, little bee, you are so beautiful.
Yellow and black, you are so beautiful.
You love the flower.
The flower loves you.
Flying around.
We all love you, too.

Chant and Song Lyrics

7 **CHANT** TR: 7.2a p.58

Happy, happy, happy.
I'm happy.
Happy, happy, happy.
I'm happy.

Sad, sad, sad.
I'm sad.
Sad, sad, sad.
I'm sad.

Happy, happy, happy.
Sad, sad, sad.
Happy, happy, happy.
Sad, sad, sad.

7 **SONG** TR: 7.4 p.61

If You're Happy and You Know It

If you're happy and you know it,
clap your hands.
If you're happy and you know it,
clap your hands.
If you're happy and you know it,
if you're happy and you know it,
if you're happy and you know it,
clap your hands.

If you're angry and you know it,
stamp your feet.
If you're angry and you know it,
stamp your feet.
If you're angry and you know it,
if you're angry and you know it,
if you're angry and you know it,
stamp your feet.

If you're sad and you know it,
cry out loud. Boo hoo!
If you're sad and you know it,
cry out loud. Boo hoo!
If you're sad and you know it,
if you're sad and you know it,
if you're sad and you know it,
cry out loud. Boo hoo!

If you're tired and you know it,
yawn out loud. Yaaaawn!
If you're tired and you know it,
yawn out loud. Yaaaawn!
If you're tired and you know it,
if you're tired and you know it,
if you're tired and you know it,
yawn out loud. Yaaaawn!

Chant and Song Lyrics

8   **CHANT** TR: 8.2   p.66

Car. Car.
I'm in a car.
Car. Car.
Look at my car.
Beep beep beep beep.

Boat. Boat.
I'm in a boat.
Boat. Boat.
Look at my boat.
Splash splash splash splash.

Aeroplane. Aeroplane.
I'm in an aeroplane.
Aeroplane. Aeroplane.
Look at my aeroplane.
Whooooshhhhhhh.

8   **SONG** TR: 8.4   p.69
Tiny Little Boat

Oh, once there was a tiny little boat.
Oh, once there was a tiny little boat.
Oh, once there was a tiny little boat.
It was so slow. It was so slow.
So slow.

Oh, once there was a tiny little boat.
Oh, once there was a tiny little boat.
Oh, once there was a tiny little boat.
It was so fast. It was so fast.
So fast.

Oh, once there was a tiny little car.
Oh, once there was a tiny little car.
Oh, once there was a tiny little car.
It was so slow. It was so slow.
So slow.

Oh, once there was a tiny little car.
Oh, once there was a tiny little car.
Oh, once there was a tiny little car.
It was so fast. It was so fast.
So fast.

CREDITS

Photography

Cover Kurit afshen/Shutterstock.com; **2–3** © ImagesBazaar/Brand X Pictures/Getty Images, © Greg Dale/National Geographic Image Collection, © yukihipo/iStock/Getty Images, © Julia Christe/fStop/Getty Images, © Anadolu Agency/Getty Images, © Tongho58/Moment/Getty Images, © Aleksandr Romanov, © Armend Nimani/AFP/Getty Images; **8–9** © ImagesBazaar/Brand X Pictures/Getty Images; **9** (tl) © Dorling Kindersley ltd/Alamy Stock Photo, (tc1) © PhotosIndia.com LLC/Alamy Stock Photo, (tc2) © Erik Von Weber/Photodisc/Getty Images, (tr) © John Kasawa/Shutterstock.com, (bl) © Wilawan Khasawong/Alamy Stock Photo, (bc) © hkeita/Shutterstock.com, (br) © Bjarte Rettedal/Photodisc/Getty Images; **10** (tl) © Derek Croucher/Alamy Stock Photo, (tc1) © Zentilia/Shutterstock.com, (tc2) © Andrew Burgess/Shutterstock.com, (tr) © Christophe Testi/Dreamstime.com, (bl) © Lucie Lang/Shutterstock.com, (bc) © Venus Angel/Shutterstock.com, (br) © Feng Yu/Shutterstock.com; **12** (tr) © Bert Pijs/NIS/Minden Pictures, (c) © twomeows/Moment/Getty Images, (br) © Phil Savoie/NPL/Minden Pictures; **15** (br) © 2015 Cengage Learning; **16** © Greg Dale/National Geographic Image Collection; **17** (tl) Jana Götze/EyeEm/Getty Images, (tc) kubowa1/Shutterstock.com, (tr) Sergiy Kuzmin/Shutterstock.com, (bl) samyaoo/Flickr/Getty Images, (bc1) Sergey Galushko/Alamy Stock Photo, (bc2) Jose Luis Pelaez Inc/DigitalVision/Getty Images, (br) cocorophotos/Bloomimage/Corbis; **20–21** MihailUlianikov/iStock/Getty Images; **22–23** © Alexandr79/Shutterstock.com; **22** (c) Bloomimage/Corbis, (bl) Classic Collection/Shotshop GmbH/Alamy Stock Photo, (br) Fuse/Corbis/Getty Images; **23** (br) © 2015 Cengage Learning; **24–25** © yukihipo/iStock/Getty Images; **25** (tl) Krataipanarak/Shutterstock.com, (tc) Liudmila Ermolenko/Shutterstock.com, (tr) foodfolio/Alamy Stock Photo, (bl) Fotosearch/Superstock, (bc1) Africa Studio/Shutterstock.com, (bc2) Roxana Bashyrova/Shutterstock.com, (br) Chekameeva Vera/Shutterstock.com; **26** (c) © Anzalone & Avarella Studios, (cr) Shebeko/Shutterstock.com; **28** © Grove Pashley/Photodisc/Getty Images; **30** (bl) Shebeko/Shutterstock.com, (bc1) showice/Shutterstock.com, (bc2) prapass/Shutterstock.com, (br) Somchai Som/Shutterstock.com; **31** (br) © 2015 Cengage Learning; **32–33** © Julia Christe/fStop/Getty Images; **33** (tl) Joel Sartore/National Geographic Image Collection, (tc) Zoltan Tougas/Shutterstock.com, (tr) Volodymyr Burdiak/Shutterstock.com, (bl) Martin Ruegner/Radius Images/Getty Images, (bc) Jim Moore/National Geographic Image Collection, (br) Juniors/Superstock; **34** (tl) (tc) Oreste Gaspari/E+/Getty Images, (tr) Eric Isselee/Shutterstock.com, (cl) (cr) Alex Segre/Flickr/Getty Images, (c) kosam/Shutterstock.com, (bl) (bc) TTstudio/Shutterstock.com, (br) iStock.com; **36** (t) Mircea Costina/Alamy Stock Photo, (b) Davesangster/iStock/Getty Images; **37** Ewais/Shutterstock.com; **39** (br) © 2015 Cengage Learning; **41** (tl) Sergiy Kuzmin/Shutterstock.com, (tc1) PhotosIndia.com LLC/Alamy Stock Photo, (tc2) Juniors/Superstock, (cr) kubowa1/Shutterstock.com, (bl) Preto Perola/Shutterstock.com, (bc1) Zoltan Tougas/Shutterstock.com, (bc2) Christophe Testi/Dreamstime.com, (br) Chekameeva Vera/Shutterstock.com; **42–43** Anadolu Agency/Getty Images; **43** (tl) (tr) Karkas/Shutterstock.com, (tc1) olegganko/Shutterstock.com, (tc2) TerraceStudio/Shutterstock.com, (bc) Africa Studio/Shutterstock.com, (br) John Kasawa/Shutterstock.com; **46** (l) Martin Rietze/Westend61/Newscom, (r) Amaia Arozena & Gotzon Iraola/Moment/Getty Images; **47** (l) Gitanna/Shutterstock.com, (r) Ralph Lee Hopkins/National Geographic Image Collection; **48–49** Apollofoto/Shutterstock.com; **49** (br) © 2015 Cengage Learning; **50–51** Tongho58/Moment/Getty Images; **51** (tl) djgis/Shutterstock.com, (tc) Alex Hyde/NPL/Minden Pictures, (tr) Malcolm Schuyl/FLPA/Minden Pictures, (c) Peter Waters/Shutterstock.com, (bl) Johannes Kornelius/Shutterstock.com, (br) David Liittschwager/National Geographic Image Collection; **54** (c) tenra/iStock/Getty Images, (tl) Oleksandr Chornyi/Tetra images/Getty Images, (br) Takashi Shinkai/Nature Production/Minden Pictures, **55** (c) Frédéric Collin/Moment/Getty Images, (l) Vinicius Tupinamba/Shutterstock.com, (t) Henrik Larsson/Shutterstock.com, (r) irin-k/Shutterstock.com; **57** (br) © 2015 Cengage Learning; **58–59** © Aleksandr Romanov; **59** (tl) elkor/E+/Getty Images, (tc) Liza McCorkle/E+/Getty Images, (tr) Christopher Hope-Fitch/Moment Select/Getty Images, (c) Laura Doss/Corbis, (bl) LaMartinia/Moment/Getty Images, (bc) Leren Lu/Stone/Getty Images, (br) Harold Lloyd/Flickr/Getty Images; **62** (t) jeffysurianto/RooM/Getty Images, (b) lessydoang/RooM/Getty Images; **63** (tl) greg801/E+/Getty Images, (tr) Gelpi JM/Shutterstock.com, (bl) phakimata/YAY Media AS/Alamy Stock Photo, (br) 3445128471/Shutterstock.com; **65** ((br) © 2015 Cengage Learning; **66–67** Armend Nimani/AFP/Getty Images; **67** (tl) Sergiy Serdyuk/Alamy Stock Photo, (tr) Andrey_Popov/Shutterstock.com, (cl) Zajac David/National Geographic Image Collection, (cr) ImageDB/Alamy Stock Photo, (bl) imagenavi/Getty Images, (bc) Chatchai Somwat/Shutterstock.com, (br) Rob Wilson/Shutterstock.com; **68** (tl) (tc) RTimages/Alamy Stock Photo, (tr) risteski goce/Shutterstock.com, (cl) (cr) MaximImages/Alamy Stock Photo, (c) Gemenacom/Shutterstock.com, (bl) Montgomery Martin/Alamy Stock Photo, (bc) (br) PhotosIndia.com LLC/Alamy Stock Photo; **70** (t) Andy Rouse/NPL/Minden Pictures, (b) Shannon Wild/National Geographic Image Collection, (br) Vincent384/Shutterstock.com; **73** (br) © 2015 Cengage Learning; **The Alphabet 76** (tl1) Alex Staroseltsev/Shutterstock.com, (tl2) Denis Tabler/Shutterstock.com, (tc) Eric Isselee/Shutterstock.com, (tr) Sonsedska Yuliia/Shutterstock.com, (cl1) F16-ISO100/Shutterstock.com, (cl2) nexus 7/Shutterstock.com, (cr1) (bl1) Guryanov Andrey/Shutterstock.com, (cr2) Eric Isselee/Shutterstock.com, (bl2) Africa Studio/Shutterstock.com, (bc) Alexandr Makarov/Shutterstock.com, (br1) VladSt/Shutterstock.com, (br2) Goran Bogicevic/Shutterstock.com; **77** (tl1) Mazzzur/Shutterstock.com, (tl2) Anita Patterson Peppers/Shutterstock.com, (tr1) Ramon Carretero/Shutterstock.com, (tr2) Dorling Kindersley ltd/Alamy Stock Photo, (cl1) donatas1205/Shutterstock.com, (cl2) Nick Koudis/Photodisc/Getty Images, (cr1) Maks Narodenko/Shutterstock.com, (cr2) Studio.G photography/Shutterstock.com, (bl1) ND700/Shutterstock.com, (bl2) WorldWide/Shutterstock.com, (bc) Irina Fischer/Shutterstock.com, (br1) baibaz/Shutterstock.com, (br2) prapass/Shutterstock.com; **79** (bl) Christophe Testi/Dreamstime.com; **Stickers: Unit 3** (tl) Galayko Sergey/Shutterstock.com, (tr) Preto Perola/Shutterstock.com, (cl1) donatas1205/Shutterstock.com, (cl2) Mazzzur/Shutterstock.com, (cr1) Ignatenko Sergey/Shutterstock.com, (cr2) Shebeko/Shutterstock.com; **Unit 5** (tl1) (tc) Africa Studio/Shutterstock.com, (tl2) Elena Shashkina/Shutterstock.com, (tr1) Serg64/Shutterstock.com, (tr2) Smit/Shutterstock.com, (cl) arturasker/Shutterstock.com, (c) Lana Langlois/Shutterstock.com, (cr) Ulga/Shutterstock.com; **Unit 6** (bl) irin-k/Shutterstock.com, (bc) Henrik Larsson/Shutterstock.com, (br) Vinicius Tupinamba/Shutterstock.com; **Unit 7** (tl1) (tl2) greg801/E+/Getty Images, (tr1) (tr2) Gelpi JM/Shutterstock.com, (cl1) (cl2) phakimata/YAY Media AS/Alamy Stock Photo, (cr1) (cr2) 3445128471/Shutterstock.com; **Unit 8** (tl) (tc) (tr) Shannon Wild/National Geographic Image Collection, (bl) (bc) (br) Andy Rouse/NPL/Minden Pictures.

Illustration

All illustrations are owned by © Cengage. **4–7, 21, 30, 38, 48, 56, 64, 72, 79**, Anna Hancock, Mascots, Puppets; **11, 14** © Taia Morley/Tugeau 2/Cengage; **13** © Adrienn Greta Schöneberg/Beehive Illustration/Cengage; **15, 23, 31, 39, 49, 57, 65, 73**, (tl) (tr) (bl) © Eric Larsen; **18–19, 80** © Andre Ceolin/MB Artists/Cengage; **27, 81** © Xiao Xin/illustrationweb.com; **35, 38–39, 82, Unit 4 Stickers** © Eva Garces; **40** (tl1) (tl2) (tc1) (tc2) (tr1) (tr2) (c) © Adrienn Greta Schöneberg/Beehive Illustration/Cengage; **44–45, 83** © Victoria Assanelli/www.organisart.co.uk; **48** (c) © Victoria Assanelli/www.organisart.co.uk, (bl) © Adrienn Greta Schöneberg/Beehive Illustration/Cengage; **52, 53, 56, 84** © Nikki Dyson; **60** © Peter Francis; **61, 85** © Lauren Gallagos/The CAT Agency, Inc./Cengage; **69, 86** © Corinna Ice/illustrationweb.com; **71** © Corinna Ice/illustrationweb.com; **72** (c) © Adrienn Greta Schöneberg/Beehive Illustration/Cengage; **74** © Juan Manuel Moreno/MB Artists/Cengage; **75** © Yulia Vysotskaya/Deb Wolfe LTD/Cengage; **79, Unit 1 Stickers** © Taia Morley/Tugeau 2/Cengage; **Unit 2 Stickers** © 2015 Cengage Learning.

NATIONAL GEOGRAPHIC LEARNING

National Geographic Learning,
a Cengage Company

Welcome to Our World 2 Student's Book
Second Edition

Series Editors: Joan Kang Shin, JoAnn (Jodi) Crandall
Authors: Jill Korey O'Sullivan, Joan Kang Shin
Publisher: Rachael Gibbon
Executive Editor: Joanna Freer
Senior Development Editor: Mary Whittemore
     and Kristen Keating
Director of Global Marketing: Ian Martin
Heads of Regional Marketing:
     Charlotte Ellis (Europe, Middle East and Africa)
     Justin Kaley (Asia and Greater China)
     Irina Pereyra (Latin America)
Content Project Manager: Ruth Moore
Media Researcher: Rebecca Ray
Art Director: Brenda Carmichael
Operations Support: Avi Mednick
Manufacturing Planner: Elaine Bevan
Composition: Lumina Datamatics Ltd.

For permission to use material from this text or product,
submit all requests online at **cengage.com/permissions**
Further permissions questions can be emailed to
permissionrequest@cengage.com

Welcome to Our World 2 Student's Book Second Edition
ISBN: 978-0-357-54268-2

Welcome to Our World 2 Student's Book with Online Practice
Second Edition
ISBN: 978-0-357-54308-5

National Geographic Learning
Cheriton House
North Way
Walworth Industrial Estate
Andover
UK
SP10 5BE

Locate your local office at **international.cengage.com/region**

Visit National Geographic Learning online at **ELTNGL.com**
Visit our corporate website at **www.cengage.com**

MIX
Paper from
responsible sources
FSC® C011748

Printed in the United Kingdom by Ashford Colour Press Ltd.
Print Number: 02 Print Year: 2023

1 **Table, Scissors, Crayons** Stickers

2 **Let's Play** Stickers

3 I Like Rice Stickers

WOW
I can!

4 Animals on the Farm Stickers

WOW
I can!

5 **Shorts and Jumpers** Stickers

6 **I Can See a Bee** Stickers

9 8 10

7 I'm Happy Stickers

WOW I can!

8 Boats, Cars, Bikes Stickers

WOW I can!